MARK JACKSON

BEST
ANALYSIS

TRUMP'S
INDICTMENT

The Unprecedented Indictment of Donald J.
Trump

MARK JACKSON

book. By reading this document, the reader agrees that under no circumstances is the author responsible for any losses, direct or indirect, which are incurred as a result of the use of the information contained within this document, including, but not limited to, — errors, omissions, or inaccuracies.

Table Of Contents

MARK JACKSON

INTRODUCTION

The United States is a great country. A country with over three hundred million people. The beauty of the United States comes from the diversity of the people that makes up the citizens of the United States. When we look at the United States, we see different people with different ways of life, we see different people with different ideologies, but in everything we do, in every one of our differences, we're all united in a common goal, which is to have a better country.

Over the years, we've come to witness so many issues that have come together to bring out our political differences. We see a set of people in support of a particular issue; we see another set of people strongly against a particular issue. Some citizens of the United States are conservatives; these ones find themselves aligning with the Republican party, while some people are liberal or progressive, and align with the Democrat party. Despite the different ideologies, despite our different preferences for the United States, we all want the same thing, which is a better America.

On March 30, 2023, history was made. On this day, the 45th president of the United States, in the person of Donald J. Trump, was indicted by a Manhattan grand jury for his alleged scandal relating to hush money payments made to a pornographic film actress, Stormy Daniels, during the 2016 US presidential election.

MARK JACKSON

Thus, Donald Trump became the first United States president to be indicted.

The indictment came as good news to many who believed that nobody is above the Law and that, no matter what, Donald Trump should be held accountable for his actions. Most of those that saw the indictment as good news were mainly Democrats. On the other hand, some people saw this as a move against democracy, not because they believed that Donald Trump should not be indicted nor because they believed that some people should be above the Law, but because of the timing of the indictment. To them, the timing speaks nothing other than a wide range of witch-hunts against the person of Donald Trump. These people are mainly supporters of the Republican Party.

On April 3, 2023, Donald Trump traveled from his residence in Florida to New York City, where he surrendered to the Manhattan District Attorney's office on the afternoon of April 4, 2023. On the same April 4, Manhattan District Attorney Alvin L Bragg, Jr. announced the indictment of Donald J Trump for falsifying New York business records in order to conceal damaging information and unlawful activity from American voters before and after the 2016 election. Trump was charged in the New York State Supreme Court indictment with 34 counts of falsifying Business Records in the first degree.

In Alvin Bragg's words, "The people of the State of New York allege that Donald J. Trump repeatedly and fraudulently falsified

MARK JACKSON

New York business records to conceal crimes that hid damaging information from the voting public during the 2016 presidential Election. Manhattan is home to the country's most significant business market.

We cannot allow New York businesses to manipulate their records to cover up criminal conduct. As the Statement of Facts describes, the trial of money and lies expose a pattern that, the people allege, violates one of New York's basic and fundamental business laws. As this office has done time and time again, we today uphold our solemn responsibility to ensure that everyone stands equal before the Law."

Yes, everyone stands equal before the Law. But there is a lot to Trump's indictment and some other activities of Donald J. Trump, which we will be looking at in this book.

MARK JACKSON

CHAPTER 1

WHAT TRUMP DID AND DIDN'T ON JANUARY 6

Can Trump still win the presidency in 2024? This is an interesting question that so many well-meaning Americans are asking.

It is no longer news that Trump, who is the 45th president of the United States, became the first president of the United States to be indicted. He was indicted for falsifying business records in order to conceal an affair that he was alleged to have had with Stormy Daniels. Trump was alleged to have about $130,000 to Stormy Daniels through his lawyer, and the intent was to make sure she didn't disclose what happened between the two of them. He was alleged to have gone further to manipulate his business records so as to keep this action that he took hidden from the public. While some have argued that Trump did this to save his marriage, some other people argued that he did this for political reasons. Whichever way, the question that is in the mind of so many people is, "Can Trump still win the presidency in 2024?"

Before we look at whether Trump could still win the presidency in 2024, let's look at what happened on January 6, which shook the whole country. Trump was alleged to have done certain things; he was also alleged not to have done certain things. So, what did Trump do, and what didn't Trump do on January 6?

MARK JACKSON

January 6, 2021, was a remarkable day in the political history of the United States. After the United States election, Congress is required by Law to certify electoral votes for the presidency.

According to White House phone logs obtained by January 6 committee, it was obvious that Donald Trump made some calls. In one of his calls, he spoke to Mr. Jordan, who was one of the leaders of the House effort; he was alleged to have told him to reject the results of the election. Trump was also said to have Stephen Miller, who happened to be his main speechwriter before he traveled to Ellipse to speak.

A special Secret Service agent who was detailed to the White House's political operation was told to have informed Trump that agents had spotted weapons in the crowd of supporters who had gathered at the Ellipse rally to hear him speak. The weapons were observed by law enforcement to include pistols, rifles, spears, and bear mace. Trump told staff to take the magnetometers set up to establish a secure area near where Trump was scheduled to speak, away. According to the reports, Trump wanted the crowd on the stage to be larger, and he kept saying that the armed rallygoers were not there to hurt him. Trump finally began his speech at around 12 pm. He repeated so many of the things he had been saying about the election for months. He then told the then-vice president, Mr. Pence, to help him overturn the election. Trump then went further to encourage the crowd; in Trump's words, "If you don't fight like hell, you're not going to have a country anymore. We're going to

MARK JACKSON

try and give them the kind of pride and boldness that they need to take back our country. The Democrats are hopeless; they never vote for anything. Not even one vote. But we're going to try and give our Republicans the weak ones because the strong ones don't need any of our help. We're going to try and give them the kind of pride and boldness that they need to take back our country."

There was also a testimony about how Trump allegedly assaulted his Secret Service bodyguard and how he tried to seize the wheel of an armored SUV. He demanded that the Secret Service agent should drive him to the Capitol, where an armed mob of his supporters was assaulting police officers and breaching security defenses in hopes of preventing Congress from certifying Joe Biden's election win. He then grabbed the car's steering wheel and lunged at the throat of a Secret Service agent while trying to get his way (this account lacks solid proof). After the whole incident, Trump returned to the White House and went to the dining room where he always stayed to watch television. According to the testimony that was given by different people who saw what happened and had to testify before the January 6 select committee, Trump spent a lot of time watching coverage of the riot on Fox News. Trump's photographer was not allowed to take pictures of Trump watching the riotous mob of his supporters assaulting police officers and then invading the Capitol. The police had a hard time trying to keep them off and bring them under control, but this proved a very difficult thing to do as the mob continued pushing and struggling to make their way. There are some videos that show a different story, as some police actually led some of the crowds

MARK JACKSON

into the Capitol. They now had to take the vice president out, and the congress members had to start looking for safety. Trump was informed about this by Tommy Tommy Tuberville. Almost an hour later, Trump then came on Twitter and made a tweet with respect to the incident. He wrote thus in his tweet:

"I am asking for everyone at the U. S Capitol to remain peaceful. No violence! Remember, we are the Party of Law & Order - respect the Law and our great men and women in Blue. Thank you!"

At around 4:03 pm, Trump then went to the White House Rose Garden to record a video calling for an end to the riot. Now, there was a written script for this speech, but Trump refused to read from the script. The script was written by his advisers, but he went on to address the rioters off the script. He told them that he knew that they were hurt because the election had been stolen, and he then asked them to go home. In his words, "We have to have peace. We have to have Law and order. We have to respect our great people in Law and order. We don't want anybody hurt. It's a very tough period of time. There's never been a time like this where such a thing happened where they could take it away from all of us - from me, from you, from our country. This was a fraudulent election, but we can't play into the hands of these people. We have to have peace. So go home. We love you. You are very special. You have seen what happens. You see the way others are treated; that is so bad and so evil. I know how you feel, but go home, and go home in peace," Trump said.

Trump's video drew widespread criticism. Despite all that he said, a lot of people pointed out that he failed to condemn the violence his supporters unleashed while trying to champion his course. He was criticized by a lot of people who believed that his action fueled the whole issue. Some people believe that if he had asked the people to go home on time, the incident could have been avoided, but he didn't. He waited until they made they obstructed the legitimate process and caused a lot of damage before he was able to tell them to go home, and even when he now had to tell them to go home, he failed to address the violence with which they decided to push for their course. The issue wasn't that they were protesting. The issue was that they were violent in their protest, they had dangerous weapons at their disposal, and this made them even more deadly.

While the widespread criticism was going on, Trump felt the need to come to Twitter around 6:01 pm to praise the rioters. In his tweet, he went on and said thus: "These are the things and events that happen when a sacred landslide election victory is so unceremoniously and viciously stripped away from great patriots who have been badly and unfairly treated for so long. Go home with love and in peace. Remember this day forever!"

Trump's tweet, even after the widespread criticism, showed that he still didn't feel the need to address the action that was taken by his supporters. This also drew more widespread criticism towards Trump. It was believed that if he had acted the way he ought to have acted, maybe, some of the damages that were carried out that day would have been avoided.

MARK JACKSON

CHAPTER 2

TRUMP'S MAJOR ACCOMPLISHMENTS AS PRESIDENT

Despite some of the things that some people who are not Trump's supporters would say against the 45th president of the United States, it is worth noting that Donald Trump was able to make a lot of accomplishments during the time he was the president of the United States. Below are some of the accomplishments of Donald Trump when he was the president of the United States:

1. Unprecedented economic boom:

Donald Trump was one of the presidents of the United States that was able to bring about a lot of growth in the economy. There are several packages in the United States to assist people who are going through a very difficult time. These packages made a major difference in household wages. These packages have been very helpful and have made America become one of the countries that have the interest of its citizens at heart. While these packages had proven to be very helpful, it is also worth noting that these packages never offered permanent solutions to the problems of some Americans.

The best way to touch the lives of the very low-income Americans and those Americans who literally earn nothing is by bringing about a boost to the economy, and this was something that Donald

Trump was able to achieve in the four years he was the president of the United States.

During the time that Donald Trump was the president of the United States, his administration was able to stimulate the production of jobs. When people have a job that helps them to pay for and take care of their needs, they wouldn't have to depend on government assistance. There is also this issue of having a high rate of crimes when people are unemployed. A person that ends up losing their job might have a family to take care of; this person has their own needs, which they have to take care of, and they have a lot of bills that they must pay. If they don't have a job, there is just no possible way for them to be able to offset most of these bills. Most of them will have to live a life of restrictions.

Some of these people eventually decide to go overboard and do whatever they can to get that very stuff that they're so much in desperate need of. This is where you see some people breaking into people's houses to steal their stuff when they're not around. This is where you see some people walk into people's stores and rob them of their day's eatrnings; this is when you see certain people take the risk of walking into a bank and carrying out a robbery against the bank. A lot of people decide to go about trying out illegal activities to make a living when they're subjected to the situation of no job. Some people are able to get a job, but even after working long hours, they don't get enough money to meet up with their basic needs, and they don't get enough cash to take care of their basic responsibilities. Some of these people decide to go into crime too.

MARK JACKSON

Of course, there is no excuse for one to decide to go into crime; we're just trying to say that a high rate of poverty has resulted in people going into crime. But Trump's administration was able to go through the broad route to be able to tackle the issue of poverty, and they did this by bringing about growth in the economy. **According to an article on Trump's White House archives,** about 7 million jobs were created during Trump's time as the president of the United States, and this was three times what government experts had projected.

Around the time Trump was the president of the United States, the middle class was among the people that made a lot of gains in his administration as the president of the United States. **According to the findings by CBS News,** Middle-Class family income increased by nearly $7,000. This was more than five times the gains during the entire previous administration that was in existence before Trump came in as the president of the United States.

For over half a century, the United States has been battling the issue of the high unemployment index. The different governments that kept coming in continued to struggle to see if they could bring down the index, but it kept proving to be a difficult thing to do. When Donald Trump came in, he was able to do something about the unemployment index. The unemployment rate reached 3.5 percent; this was the lowest that had ever been recorded in fifty years. It was something that his predecessors couldn't achieve. For forty months in a row, there were more job openings than job hirings because the economy was made favorable for this. A lot of

MARK JACKSON

people were opening their own businesses, and we know what this means; it means they would have to later employ more people. More Americans reported being employed than ever before in the Trump administration. Nearly 160 million people reported being employed during the Trump administration. Jobless claims were able to hit a nearly 50 years low. The number of people that were claiming unemployment insurance as a share of the population went to its lowest on record. Incomes rose in every single metro area in the United States; this happened for the first time in nearly thirty to fifty years.

2. Delivered a future of greater opportunity for citizens of all backgrounds:

In the United States, there has always been a belief that there are a certain group of people in society whom the system seems to have favored getting a better life than people of other groups. In the aspect of employment, for example, there had always been a belief that the rate of unemployment was higher in certain races or a certain group of people, but Trump's administration came in and further brought this to an all-time low record. Unemployment rates for African Americans, Hispanic Americans, Asian Americans, Native Americans, people with disabilities, veterans, those without high school diplomas, and many other groups of people went to an all-time low. Every group of United States citizens recorded an all-time rate low record in unemployment. Now, there had also been the belief that women were most likely to face unemployment than their male counterparts in the United States. When Trump was the president of the United States, unemployment for women hit its lowest rate, and it was the first time in almost a century. A lot of women became employed during Donald Trump's administration than the way it was with those who were the president of the United States before Donald Trump. Before Donald Trump became the president of the United States, the population of United States citizens that depended on food stamps was very alarming. But when Donald Trump became the president of the United States, he was able to stimulate changes through his policies that went on to help in promoting the standard of living of most Americans. About 7 million people were lifted off food stamps during the time Donald Trump was the president of the United States.

African Americans had always recorded a high poverty rate in the United States, followed by Hispanic Americans, but the Trump administration was able to reduce the number of African Americans and Hispanic Americans that were struggling with poverty. This became evident in the number of African Americans that became homeowners during the time Donald Trump became the president of the United States. For people to become homeowners, they should at least have had enough to solve their most pressing problems. It is always natural for humans to try to solve their most pressing problems before they would pay attention to other problems that have to do with their comfort. An average human being is much interested in what to eat, simple stuff to wear, paying their kids' tuition fees, paying the electricity bill, paying the water bill, and other very essential bills that they sure

MARK JACKSON

can't just do without. They only start making attempts to own properties when they know they've become comfortable enough to provide most of their basic needs. Before people start thinking about owning a house, they must have been able to have enough to the point that they wouldn't be considered as people who are struggling with poverty. The Trump administration lifted a lot of African Americans from poverty; the Trump administration offered them more jobs, it offered them more opportunities to own their own businesses, and they were able to save enough to own their own house. African American homeownership when Trump was the president increased from 41.7 percent to 46.4 percent.

According to Forbes, during the time Donald Trump was the president of the United States, the bottom 50 percent of American households saw 40 percent increase in net worth. Wages rose fastest for low-income and blue-collar workers, as there was about a 16 percent pay increase. Of course, companies and businesses would be able to pay people more if they happen to be earning more. When people start earning more, they would be able to employ more people, and they would be able to effect wage increases. Most businesses want to pay high wages, but because they might not be earning as much as they had projected, they might have to stick to paying low wages and salaries to be able to maintain their profit margin.

But the Trump administration kind of saw a lot of businesses doing better than they used to do in the past, so the pay increase was effectively implemented. As a result of how Trump's administration was able to effect a lot of positive changes, income inequality fell for two straight years and by the largest amount in over a decade. A lot of Americans that had a life more difficult for them during past administrations experienced better living when Donald Trump was the president of the United States. Those that were seen as the lowest citizens because of their earnings found themselves going up in their financial status.

One of the big problems a lot of people, especially those that were considered the low earners, were facing was the problem of not being able to have any savings. When people have savings, there is no limit to how much they would be able to get better with their lives. When people are saving, they would be able to develop because, in most cases, self-development comes with spending some cash.

So, some people have always found themselves revolving around a particular spot. No matter what they did to get better from their situation, they always still found themselves struggling with the same things which they had always struggled with. These people knew that their states were not good, they knew what they could do to get better from their low state, but they couldn't do it because their daily lives were making it so difficult and impossible for them to be able to make any savings off what they were earning. Some of these people had other people in their lives who should be employed, but these people were not gainfully employed, so they had to depend so much on them. They couldn't just save anything as a result of this; they continued to remain at the same level, year in and year out. When Trump's administration came in, a lot of people that found themselves in this state were able to make moves. They had been relegated to this situation for a very long time, but Trump's administration was able to pull them out of it. Some of them were able to save some of their money and were able to invest in buying properties. Some of them were able to save some money and were able to start their own businesses; these ones that were able to start their own businesses saw life becoming better for them, and they were also able to employ some other people who didn't have a job.

A lot of people that had always found themselves at the bottom during the previous administrations before Donald J. Trump became the president found themselves going up to the ladder of riches.

3. Brought Industries back to the United States.

Before Donald Trump came to the United States, industries in the United States weren't areas in which people were thinking about investing. Factories weren't where people wanted to invest in. Of course, there were a lot of factories; there were a lot of industries before Trump's administration. But these factories and industries had the problem of expansion. Some of them already had this aspiration of expansion, but they just couldn't bring this into materialization because of policies of the previous administrations that were there before Trump. Around when Donald Trump came into office, the policies he brought to the table stimulated a lot of growth in industries and factories. Some factories and industries saw themselves recording all-time high-profit margins. People only spend when the economy looks favorable. When the economy looks favorable, people find themselves earning more, and as a result of this, they try to spend more. But when people don't earn much as a result of the economy not looking favorable, they make the best use of the little they've; they'll also end up boycotting some products, even if they need them. As a result of this, some industries and factories will also be affected because the demand for their products and services will also go low. When factories are recording very low interest, the possibility of expansion becomes low, and the possibility of employing more people continues going low. But when factories find themselves recording high demand, they make a lot of profit; they start thinking about expanding. Expansion always results in to increase in the rate of employment.

Trump's administration brought a lot of expansion in existing factories. The Trump administration triggered some people into going into their own factory businesses. A lot of manufacturing companies sprung forth during Trump's administration. A lot of construction work sprung forth during Trump's administration.
The number of people that wanted to own properties increased, so it triggered an increase in construction jobs.
Trump's administration created more than 1.2 million manufacturing and construction jobs.

MARK JACKSON

According to a report on Forbes's official website, Small business optimism broke a 35-year-old record in 2018. In 2018, Trump was still the president of the United States. This achievement was a result of how his policies stimulated growth around the bottom. A lot of people that continued becoming poorer during the previous administration saw a boost during the time of Trump's administration, and some of them became business owners.

4. Rural parts of the United States had always been the bedrock of food production in the United States but had faced the low level of modernization in previous administrations that existed before the time of Donald Trump.

Around when Donald Trump was campaigning to become the president of the United States, his campaign promises targeted those in the rural areas of the United States. His campaign promises promised to bring about improvement in what had always been a norm in the previous administrations before he came in as the president of the United States. Some rural communities had always felt like they were abandoned as most of the government policies seemed to be targeting those in modern areas. As a result of this, there has always been a high rate of emigration in rural communities. Many people have always preferred to emigrate from rural communities to urban communities because they believe that urban communities have a better standard of living than rural areas, they believe that life is better in urban communities than in rural communities, they believe that there were better job opportunities in the urban communities than in the rural communities. Some people had been in rural communities and had been trying to bring about growth in their lives, but things never worked out for them, so they had to migrate to urban communities. The rate of emigration from urban communities to rural communities had always continued to go all-time low because how people believed that they had a better life to live in the urban communities than the rural communities. As a result of this, some urban communities have always recorded overcrowding and overpopulation.

The implication of this is that the rate of unemployment in some urban communities started going up. When you've so many people moving into urban communities, some of them were already unemployed and were moving into the urban community with a plan to get a job. Some people already staying in the urban community were already done with college and were looking for better jobs. All of these people fused together to increase the rate of unemployment in urban communities. A lot of people were just going after a few jobs. This had always been the reality in most urban communities in the United States. The white-collar jobs were very competitive because there were a lot of people searching for them. Some of these people that were searching for these white-collar jobs moved in from rural communities, while some of them were already staying in urban communities.

The Trump administration did something to bring about some degree of balance. A lot of people will continue to move to rural communities if they don't feel that their lives in rural communities will become better. Look at it this way, most of the people living in rural communities own their own properties. Some of them are living in their family properties. The cost of living in these areas should at least be targeted to be all-time low, but these people still have to leave everything behind and go to urban cities because they want to bring about growth in their lives. Of course, they're comfortable in their rural communities, but their lives aren't improving. If they had to remain in these rural communities, they would most likely never become millionaires. A lot of people had to move to other places with better opportunities. Trump's administration was able to reduce the rate of emigration from rural communities to urban communities.

According to WhiteHouse.gov, During the time Trump was the president of the United States, he signed an executive order on modernizing the Regulatory Framework for Agricultural Biotechnology products. This brought innovative new technologies to market in American farming and agriculture. A lot of people in rural areas that had always felt discouraged in investing in agriculture suddenly picked interest in agriculture. More food was produced, and more employment was produced. Some people living in urban areas decided to migrate to rural areas so that they would invest in rural areas as a result of the policies of the Trump administration.

Trump's administration targeted the rural economy. A lot of effort was made by Trump's administration to change what had been the norm in the previous administrations. The rural economy had always been known to be low, with the level of investments being low and the level of job creation in rural areas being low. Most rural jobs don't even pay much like the jobs in the urban areas because there is this belief that the cost of living in the rural area is low, so the job pay should kind of reflect the economic situation of the area. Trump had an agenda to improve the standard of living in rural communities. He did a lot of campaigns in rural communities, and when he became the president of the United States, he stayed true to the promises he made to most rural communities. The Trump administration strengthened America's rural economy by investing over $1.3 billion through the Agriculture Department's ReConnect program to bring high-speed broadband infrastructure to rural America. This went further to affect the lives of those living in these rural areas in a positive manner. Their earnings went higher, and their savings went higher.

5. **Achieved a record-breaking economic comeback by rejecting blanket lockdowns:**

The pandemic that was forced on the world as a result of Covid 19 brought about a lot of changes in the kind of life which so many people had come to get used to. Humans have always been used to living their free life. There are a lot of things a living human already has planned out for their day. They would go out for their dates, they'll go out for their work, they'll take their kids to school and bring them back from school, some would go to school, some would go get some groceries, some would go to the park, there was just a lot of routines which humans had come to get used to as their daily life, and these routines had come to shape our lives,

MARK JACKSON

these routines had come to shape what we find to be fun and what we've come to find bothering. Now, when Covid 19 came, no one knew that it was going to cost the world as much as it did. It was looked down on, but by the time it started spreading, the reality shook a lot of people. At some point, the government of the world was forced to make tough decisions that would cost a lot of people the routines that had come to become part of their lives.

The decision was to impose a long down; this was to make sure that the virus was made to stop spreading. It was believed that if the possibility of people meeting and having contacts could be reduced, then it could be possible to bring about a stop to the spread of the virus. It started with the imposition of a partial lockdown. The partial lockdown didn't seem to stop anything; a total lockdown was declared. This saw a shutdown in most of the public places in the United States. The citizens of the United States were forced to live the kind of life to which they had never gotten exposed to. It was so difficult as a lot of people found themselves struggling with depression. They couldn't go out there to live their normal lives; they couldn't go out there to meet their friends; they couldn't go out there to earn money; they just couldn't go out there to do what they loved doing.

The citizens of a lot of countries went through a lot during the time of the pandemic. A lot of people were locked up in their homes with nothing to eat and no government assistance. The third world countries were believed to record the lowest rate of mortality as a result of Covid 19 infection, but a lot of people died from starvation and depression because of no government assistance. The United States faired well under the watch of Donald Trump. An October 2020 Gallup survey found 56 percent of Americans said they were better off during a pandemic than four years prior. Despite the issues that were thrown on the world by the pandemic, a lot of Americans believed their lives were better off during the pandemic than four years before the pandemic set in. During the third quarter of 2020, the economy grew at a rate of 33.2 percent; this was, in fact, the most rapid GDP growth ever recorded in the United States.

Over the world, some countries are still suffering the effect of the Covid 19 pandemic even to date. The rate of unemployment in most countries continued to surge higher, and the poverty rate in some countries became all high record-breaking. These actually kind of triggered the increase in crime in some countries. Of course, the United States was among the country that went through all those economic issues that were brought forth as a result of the Covid 19 pandemic; in the United States, there was retrenchment of staff in some companies who were struggling to maintain their profit margin, people found themselves losing their jobs around the time which they believed they needed their job the most to survive. A lot of savings were taken to zero dollars because so many people had to depend on the money which they had saved. Some of the money which these people had saved where money for making investments, and some were money that they wanted to use and run a particular project. People were just pushed to the wall as a result of how the Covid 19 pandemic stretched their family economy. But despite all of these, the United States was able to make a quick comeback, despite all the things the United States went through when the Covid 19 pandemic was at its peak, and this was possible because of the measures that were put in place by Donald Trump. Before Donald Trump finished his tenure as the United States president, he was able to add back about 12 million jobs; this was more than half the jobs that were lost because of the Covid 19 pandemic. Jobs recovered 23 times faster during the time that Trump was the president of the United States, more than the way it did during the time of the previous administrations.

A lot of people think that a great population of the United States would have to pay the price of post-Covid 19 lockdowns. We kept hearing people saying that 'life would never remain the same again. Of course, there were several reasons for this statement, but one of these several reasons was because of the level of unemployment that experts had projected would hit the United States; after the lockdown, people were surprised at how quickly they bounced back to their normal way of living. Even those that were fired from their job during the lockdown either found another well-paying job or were called back to their workplace. Before Donald Trump left office as the president of the United States, unemployment fell to 6.7 percent in December 2020; this was from a pandemic peak of 14.7 percent in April. This achievement surpassed the expectation of beating over 10 percent unemployment by the end of 2020.

The previous administration that came in before Trump had struggled a lot with unemployment. They did a lot of things to be

MARK JACKSON

able to curb unemployment; they put several measures which they believed would be able to bring down the percentage of those unemployed. It took the previous administration that was in power before Donald Trump about 49 months before they were able to effect a fall from 10 percent to 7 percent in the population of the unemployed in the United States. While this took the previous administration 49 months to achieve, it only to Donald Trump three months to achieve. It was something no president in the United States had been able to achieve at a very wrong time.

It is on record that from April 2020, the Hispanic unemployment rate fell by 9.6 percent. Asian-American unemployment fell by 8.6 percent, while African American unemployment fell by 6.8 percent. These were very big achievements because if the population of these people that were able to become employed had to remain unemployed because of the issues that were brought up by the Covid 19 pandemic, the situation in the United States would have been very bad. But Trump was able to make a quick comeback.

Around April 2020, about 53 percent of businesses were open, but by the end of the year, about 80% of small businesses opened. This was so high when compared with what experts had projected. The reason for this was that small businesses were able to build very high confidence. People only build confidence when they see that the ground has this look that things are going to work out for them. These people that built their confidence saw the measures which the Trump administration was putting in to make the economy even better than it had been in the past. Now, around

MARK JACKSON

this time, one very significant thing that was noticed was that home building started going high. The confidence of homebuilders went to an all-time high. A lot of homes were built around the end of 2020, this was a period that so many experts had thought would have an all-time low record of homebuilders, but the record went very high. And, while the record of home builders went high, sales of homes went very high. Sales of homes hit their highest reading since December 2006.

Almost immediately after the lockdown, there was a boom in manufacturing. Manufacturing optimism almost got doubled as industries and factories scaled up their manufacturing strength.

There is this particular thing about demand. When a lot of people are demanding something, the implication is that the price of this particular thing which so many people are demanding will naturally go high. This is because, for a single commodity, there are possibilities that up to five people would be trying to get their hands on it. Think about it this way, if suddenly, it happens that there is only one ball in the United States and several parents in the United States want to buy a ball for their kid. If all of these parents went to the market and found out that they could only buy from the remaining one ball, the price of the ball would normally go high because the person selling would most likely try to capitalize on the fact that there are a lot of people trying to buy, to make more cash. The point is that when there are a lot of people that are trying to buy a product, there is a high chance that the price of that product will go high. This was exactly what was reflected in home prices towards the end of 2020. Look at it this way; common sense would make one imagine that home prices would go to an all-time low around the end of 2020 because of the Covid 19 lockdown. The reason for this is that so many property owners would have gone broke and would now be looking for how to sell off some of their properties so that they would be able to make some cash that would help them bounce back on their feet.

The idea was that those that have like two, three, or even more houses would have to sell their houses so that they would be able to raise some money which would help them to bring about a balance in their lives. When you look at this from another angle, you'll also notice that even as there were projections that the percentage of property owners that would want to sell their properties would go all-time high, the percentage of those that would be available to buy these properties would most likely be low because a lot of people went through a lot of financial crisis during the Covid 19 lockdown. So, when you've so many people trying to sell their properties, and then a very small amount of people are available to buy, what should happen? The price of homes would just go down to an all-time low. Some people might even have to sell without considering their profit. But this was not what happened. Trump's administration defiled all economic permutation and reasoning in the housing sector. Despite the fact that there were more people who wanted to sell homes, there were even more people who were ready to buy.

MARK JACKSON

According to an article found in Trump's White House archives, Household net worth in 2020 rose from %7.4 trillion in the second quarter to %112 trillion; this was just too high; it was actually an all-time high record. It was achieved by no other but Donald J. Trump.

Around when the world was on lockdown. The United States was having a lot of problems with the lockdown. Even Trump, before the lockdown, took a stand that he wasn't going to allow a lockdown to hold, but he was pressured into it as there were a lot of criticisms coming from different angles on how the president was undermining people's safety. He had to give in to pressure, but even as the lockdown lingered, Trump continued to make it known about the need to call off the lockdown. The United States was one of the first countries to call off the lockdown. By the time the United States called off the lockdown, some other countries in the world had followed.

The United States rejected crippling lockdowns that crushed economies and inflicted countless public health harms. Yes, there were a lot of health concerns with regard to the lockdown; this was apart from the economic concern. People were so depressed that their mental health went into jeopardy. We saw people not dying from the virus, which we were running from, but from depression, domestic violence, and other vices. The economic effect now went on to add more pain to the masses. The United States safely reopened its economy; this was triggered by the efforts made by Trump. The effect of this was that the economy was able to

MARK JACKSON

bounce back so quickly. To this day, business confidence in the United States is higher than business confidence in any European country in the world. This was a result of the measures that were taken by Trump. After the lockdown, Trump's administration was able to stabilize America's financial markets with the establishment of a number of Treasury Department support facilities at the Federal Reserve.

6. Tax relief for the middle class:

One of the most important ways government uses in making its revenue is through tax. Tax is very important to the government because, through the revenue made from tax, the government is able to carry out most of its developmental projects. When you look at the United States, you'll get to see that the government has several schemes going on. These schemes cost the government a lot of money. One of the ways through which government makes its money is true tax. There are a lot of people that are under the employ of the government.

The government has several institutions scattered in different parts of the country. These institutions need a lot of money for them to continue working. Part of the money that is used to keep these institutions running is often coming from the money paid by taxpayers. So, without tax, the government will most likely find it very difficult to be able to raise money that would be used in funding most of their projects, and if the government is not funding projects, the country will be in a big problem. So, for the country to be moving fine, there is a need to fund projects, and for projects to be funded, there is a need to get taxes from the people living in the country, both citizens and none citizens. Now, we've continued hearing about how some government policies have continued to discourage people from investing in the economies of some countries. When we hear stuff like this, most times, it has to do with the kind of tax the government is getting from these people who have the intention of investing in the economy or these people who have already started investing in the economy. There are governments that impose a high tax on people. Now, when people want to invest, they've several options. When you see foreign investors trying to invest in a country, these people have options of several other countries that they could go to and then establish their investment. One of the things that affect their options is tax. When a country is known to have very high tax rates, a lot of foreign investors would be discouraged from investing in countries like this.

Trump knew that for the country to record a high rate of investment, the people had to be encouraged to invest, and the people had to be made to save some of their money so that they would invest them. By the time these people invest, they will also end up creating more jobs for people who are still struggling to get jobs. As a result of this idea, Trump's idea took a serious look at the tax system and agreed that it was very important to do something about it. It made no sense that the government would be making a lot on tax, and most of the money they're making from the tax would be going on food stamps because more people are continuing to find it difficult to afford their own food. It was better to stimulate these people so that they would have more money, go off the food stamps, create jobs, and also help in taking more people off the food stamps. This was one of the ways Trump was able to take a lot of people off food stamps. He made life better for them through tax cuts.

According to an article found in Trump's White House archives, Trump's administration signed the Tax Cuts and Jobs Act. This happened to be the largest tax reform package in the history of the United States. There was never an administration that was able to achieve this landslide. The Trump administration took this direction because Trump had always said that Americans would always come first before anything, and he remained to his words. A typical family of four that was earning around %75,000 had their tax bill slashed into half, and they received an income tax cut of over %2,000; this was in addition to the fact that over 6 million American workers received wage increases, bonuses, and increased benefits. These were a result of the tax cuts that were carried out by the Trump administration.

Now, there was this tax on Estate, which had oftentimes been seen as being unfair. This tax caused a lot of issues for Americans. The past administrations had ignored it. But when Trump came in, he virtually eliminated the unfair Estate Tax or Death Tax.
When you go to developed countries all over the world, one of the common peculiarities is the high rate of tax in these countries. Some countries have very tax rates, and it has become so common to continue reading articles and watching videos of people

complaining online about the tax system in such countries. Some countries have this policy of taking a large chunk of people's earnings on tax, thereby making it so difficult for them to live the kind of life they want to live and invest in the economy.

Some developed countries are not recording enough growth in industrialization because of the high rate of tax in these countries. These countries always present this idea that they depend so much on tax to make revenue than other possible areas. People who would make positive impacts on the economy of these developed countries with very high tax rates find it difficult to migrate to that country because of the tax they would have to be paying. When Donald Trump became the president of the United States, he had to cut the business tax rate from 35 percent to 21 percent. Thirty-five percent was part of the highest tax percentage in developed countries. It was as if businesses were just spending all their profit on tax, but Trump's administration brought an end to this by making 40 percent cuts in business tax.

The Trump administration made things easier for small businesses. While small businesses were dying in other countries, small businesses in the United States were striving; these were a result of the policies made by Donald Trump. Small businesses can now deduct 20 percent of their business income. Businesses can now deduct 100 percent of the cost of their capital investments in the year the investment is made. These were policies that were put in place by the Trump administration that eventually offered a lot of boost to businesses.

MARK JACKSON

Since the passage of tax cuts, the share of state wealth held by the bottom half of households has increased, while the share held by the 1 percent decreased. And as we know, there are more people at the bottom of households than at the top of households. This showed that a lot of lives were made better by Trump's administration.

As a result of the tax cuts that were brought about by Trump's administration, over 400 companies announced bonuses and wage increases. The 40 percent tax cuts increased their revenue, and this was reflected in how they started treating their staff and what their staff was getting in return for their services. Over 400 companies also announced new hires in the United States. There are companies that are struggling with understaffing. This was because they were struggling to maintain their profit margin. The tax they were paying was so high, and they didn't want to pull out from the economy, so to be able to survive and remain there, they had to understaff their facilities. This meant that the working conditions they offered to their staff were unfavorable, but some of their staff still had to stay because they wanted to remain employed and because there were no other companies around that had better offers. Other companies around were having the same issues because of the high tax. But Donald Trump came in and changed what used to be the narrative. Donald Trump came in and brought a cut, this now made companies have some degree of comfort, and they now had to hire more hands to bring a balance in their staff. Now, this now improved the working conditions of the staff

MARK JACKSON

working in their facilities. It is important to also note that there were companies that started making new investments as a result of the tax cut. The tax cut increased their earnings; the tax cut made it possible for them to start up a new investment with little tax attached to it. As a result of these new investments, new hires were made. This kind of brought about an increase in employment.

As a result of the tax cut, over %1.5 trillion was repatriated into the United States from overseas. Lower investment costs and higher capital returns led to faster growth in the middle class and real wages. One thing that these led to was that the United States was able to be ahead in its international competition with other countries when it came to investments and revenue making.

7. Brought more money for Americans.

The implication of most of the policies which were made by Donald Trump was that Americans now found themselves having more money in their pockets. The system was channeled towards building the individuals rather than making money off the individuals. The Trump administration was more concerned about building rich individuals rather than making money off individuals in other to make life better for the same individuals. Look at it this way when individuals get to give all the money which should have gone into their savings to the government so that the government would better the economy. By the time the government would better the economy, the same individuals will not have any money left to invest in the economy. Trump's administration was able to take little from the individual to build the economy, and the individuals, in return, had a lot left to invest in the economy, thereby making them contribute to making the economy even better; the lives of the individuals became far better than it was in the previous administrations, and they were able to make lives of others around them become better.

Deregulation had an especially beneficial impact on low-income earners in America, who spend a great part of their income on overregulation. The Trump administration was able to cut red tape in the healthcare industry, providing Americans with more affordable healthcare and saving nearly 10 percent of Americans on prescription drugs. Trump's administration was able to remove barriers to personal freedom and consumer choice in healthcare. It is on record that Trump's administration signed 16 pieces of deregulatory legislation that will result in a $40 billion increase in real annual incomes.

8. Put America first:

America has always been a country that accommodates a lot of foreign countries. When you look around the world, you'll get to see that America is the only country that has made a certain degree of positive impact in almost every country of the world, including China. When Donald Trump was making his campaign promises, he pointed out a lot of unfair standards that had been going on in the United States. These standards prioritized other countries than the United States. Trump continued saying that if he won the election, he would put America before every other country. When he eventually won the election, he did exactly what he said he was going to do.

Trump's administration imposed tariffs on hundreds of billions worth of Chinese goods to protect American jobs and stop China's abuses under Section 232 of the Trade Expansion Act of 1962 and Section 301 of the Trade Act of 1974. Trump's administration went further to direct government efforts towards putting a halt and bringing about serious consequences for China for stealing profit from American innovations and intellectual properties. While Trump's administration was making tax cuts for the Americans, Trump's administration particularly imposed tariffs on foreign aluminum and foreign steel to protect the American aluminum and steel industries. The Trump administration took action against France for its digital services tax that unfairly targeted American technology companies and then went further to launch an investigation into digital services taxes that had been adopted by ten other countries.

The Trump administration blocked illegal timber imports from Peru, thereby offering timber trade within the United States a lot of boosts. Trump's administration also approved tariffs on $1.8 billion in imports of washing machines and $8.5 billion on imports of solar panels.

The achievements made by Trump's administration in four years were so enormous that even those that weren't supporters would have to be surprised if they had to take a look at them. Trump is

MARK JACKSON

Trump. He might not be perfect, but his achievements in just one tenure as the United States president surpassed the achievements made by several other presidents that served for two terms.

MARK JACKSON

CHAPTER 3

TRUMP'S INDICTMENT

Everything sure has a first time, and so was a historical phenomenon that took place on March 30, 2023. On this day, for the first time in the history of the United States, a past president of the United States was indicted. This happened to no other person but Donald J. Trump, one of the most controversial presidents the United States had ever had in the history of its existence.

On March 30, 2023, Trump was indicted by a Manhattan grand jury for allegedly paying a pornographic film actress, Tormy Daniels, during the 2016 United States election. His indictment came with 34 felony charges of falsifying business records in the first degree.

Trump's indictment shook every nook and cranny of the United States, with different people having their own opinion about the indictment. Some people believed that it was a move in the right direction because they believed it was time for Trump to be held accountable for his too many excesses. Some other people believed that the indictment of Donald J. Trump was another calculated plan put together to put an end to his presidential race; these people believe the timing of the indictment has a lot to confirm this.

MARK JACKSON

On April 3, 2023, Trump traveled from his residence in Florida to New York City. On April 4, 2023, Trump surrendered himself to the Manhattan District Attorney's office.

Before Trump surrendered himself, there had been a lot of speculations about how Trump would be treated, whether he would be cuffed or whether his fingerprints would be taken. There were even a lot of edited pictures of him online where the creators made it look like the police were having a fight with Trump while trying to arrest him. This was another speculation as a lot of people believed that Trump wouldn't surrender and that this would most likely lead to him being forced and cuffed. But on April 4, 2023, Trump surrendered himself. Just like every other American, his fingerprints were taken, and he appeared in court with no force.

On April 4, 2023, Manhattan District Attorney Alvin L. Bragg, Jr formally announced the indictment of Donald J. Trump for falsifying business records in order to conceal damaging information and unlawful activity from American voters before and after the 2016 presidential election.

According to court documents and statements made on the record in court, from August 2015 to December 2017, Trump made some payments that he concealed through months of false business entries. The document stated that in one instance, American Media Inc. Paid $30,000 to a former Trump Tower doorman, who claimed to have a story about a child Trump had out of wedlock. In a second instance, the document stated that American Media Inc

MARK JACKSON

paid $150,000 to a woman who alleged she had a sexual relationship with Trump. When Trump directed a lawyer who then worked for the Trump Organization as Trump's special counsel to reimburse American Media Inc in cash, the Special Counsel told Trump that the payment should be made through a shell company and not by cash. However, American Media Inc declined to accept reimbursement after consulting their counsel. American Media Inc later made false entries in its business records so as to conceal the true purpose of the $150,000 payment made to the woman who alleged she had sex with Trump.

In the third instance, twelve days before the presidential general election, Trump's Special Counsel wired $130,000 to an attorney for an adult film actress through a shell corporation funded through a bank in Manhattan. The Special Counsel later pleaded guilty and served his jail term. After Trump won his election, he reimbursed the Special Counsel through a series of monthly checks. Nine of these checks were signed by Trump and were disguised as payment for legal services rendered. Thirty-four false entries were made in New York business records so as to conceal the $130,000 payment.

The indictment of Donald Trump had been speculated by so many people to have **a** political undertone; some have even said it is clear proof of the speculation that the American Judiciary w**as** attacking conservatives. Despite the different views of Americans about Trump's indictment, one thing is very certain, Trump's indictment will have **a** huge effect on the 2024 presidential election.

MARK JACKSON

MARK JACKSON

CHAPTER 4

CAN TRUMP STILL WIN THE PRESIDENCY IN 2024?

Alvin Bragg's predecessor didn't pursue Trump. There had always been some group of the American population that had always talked about Trump being pursued and prosecuted for falsifying business documents, but Bragg's predecessor didn't pursue the case. But by the time Bragg came in, the whole energy was channeled toward Trump. The most bothering thing about this is the timing of the whole thing. While the United States election is barely a year and a half away, Trump is faced with 34 separate indictments; this looks like a calculated move. Never in American history has any president or former president been indicted; of course, most of America's past presidents were not saints.

Most journalists agreed that Bragg's case lacked any meat as the indictment was unsealed at arraignment. With a clear view of the 34 separate indictments, one would see that they're all the same offense that was copied and pasted without anything new added to them.

While the judiciary has the right to make its decisions on its own on how court cases should be run, there is something about this Trump indictment that has raised a lot of questions in the mind of well-meaning Americans. The judge had to push the hearing close to the time the Republicans would be having their primaries. A

MARK JACKSON

look at this shows that there is a political agenda to stop and distract Trump from winning the primaries. Look at it this way, how will the Republican party cast its confidence on a man that is facing indictment charges in court? How will they cast their confidence in a man whom the judge could just send to jail after his trial? This kind of casts a lot of uncertainty on Trump's ambition. It just looks like the system is organized to push Trump out of the presidential race. Trump had been facing a lot of backlash from the media and from different angles. We saw how Donald Trump was banned by Twitter and Facebook for violating their community standards. About three years later, they had to free Trump's social media account because they believed it didn't violate their community standards. And now, the election is so close, an indictment was brought up to derail him, and the indictment hearing had to be pushed close to the primaries to make matters worst for Trump. The case of Stormy Daniels came up around when Trump was trying to contest his first term. This was another agenda that was pushed forward to distract the then-presidential aspirant. Trump was pressured into paying the sum to keep things hidden, and now another election is so close, and they are employing tactics to hinder him from returning to the White House.

Nobody is above the Law. But the pattern in which judges decide to pursue a case goes a long way to show if they were actually after ridding the country of crime or if they're actually pursuing a particular agenda, an agenda channeled towards attacking conservatives. The American judiciary had not really been fair to

MARK JACKSON

conservatives; this had been proved in Trump's indictment and in several other issues that had happened in the past.

DeSantis happens to be the projected opponent of Donald Trump in the quest for the position of the president of the United States under the Republican party. There will have to be a primary to determine who will be representing the Republican party in the presidential poll, but as of the time of writing, DeSantis is yet to declare his interest in running for the presidency officially. The indictment is clearly channeled towards discrediting Trump, but immediately after the indictment, Trump's rating went even higher than that of DeSantis. This now still brings us back to the question, "can Trump still win the presidency in 2024?"

The increase in Trump's rating, despite the indictment, has proved one thing, which is that the majority of the United States citizens have become aware of the agenda to push Trump out of the race. The Democrats never believed that Trump would win his first term election. In fact, they even had to give him a soft landing during debates so that they'll confuse the Republicans into believing that he would win, but he won the election. It wouldn't be right to conclude that Trump would win the election, we don't even know if he would win the primaries, but one thing we know is that Trump is a fighter; he always knows how to turn the odds into his favor, and there are high chances that he could win the 2024 presidential election.

MARK JACKSON

Citations

Bromwich, J. E., Protess, B., Rashbaum, W. K., & Gold, M. (2023a, April 5). Trump Indictment: What We Know and What Comes Next. *The New York Times*. https://www.nytimes.com/article/trump-indictment-criminal-charges.html

Chotiner, I. (2023a, April 13). Is the Trump Indictment a "Legal Embarrassment"? *The New Yorker*. https://www.newyorker.com/news/q-and-a/is-the-trump-indictment-a-legal-embarrassment

Cnn, B. K. S. J. M. J. H. a. D. C. (2023a, March 31). Donald Trump indicted by Manhattan grand jury on more than 30 counts related to business fraud. *CNN*. https://amp.cnn.com/cnn/2023/03/30/politics/donald-trump-indictment/index.html

Olson, E. (2023a, April 7). Stormy Daniels says she's not yet "vindicated" by Trump's indictment. *NPR*. https://www.npr.org/2023/04/07/1168604443/stormy-daniels-piers-morgan-interview-trump

Pengelly, M. (2023a, April 9). Trump's indictment and the return of his biggest concern: 'the women.' *Donald Trump | the Guardian*. https://amp.theguardian.com/us-news/2023/apr/09/trump-indictment-women-stormy-daniels-karen-mcdougal

MARK JACKSON

Read the full indictment against Trump. (2023a, April 8). *AP NEWS*.

https://apnews.com/article/trump-indictment-full-document-

640043319549

The indictment of Donald Trump. (2023a, April 5). *Financial Times*.

https://www.ft.com/content/c15b9672-cf4a-494d-a0c4-

314512c427d7

Widakuswara, P. (2023a, April 8). Trump Is Indicted — Now What?

https://www.voanews.com/amp/trump-is-indicted-now-what-

/7041520.html. https://www.voanews.com/amp/trump-is-

indicted-now-what-/7041520.html

Zahn, M. (2023a, April 9). Donald Trump indictment: What to know

about falsifying business records. *ABC News*.

https://abcnews.go.com/amp/US/donald-trump-indictment-

falsifying-business-records/story?id=98377002

Donald Trump pleads not guilty to 34 felony counts; indictment unsealed.

(2023, April 5). 6abc Philadelphia.

https://6abc.com/donald-trump-indicted-new-york-

grand-jury/13082721/

Italiano, L., & Snodgrass, E. (2023b, March 31). How a Trump

arrest would play out: Yes, he'll be fingerprinted. No, he

probably won't be handcuffed. *Business Insider Africa*.

https://africa.businessinsider.com/politics/how-a-trump-arrest-would-play-out-yes-hell-be-fingerprinted-no-he-

probably-wont-be/tkrjjjk

Treisman, R. (2023, March 31). What happens after Trump's

indictment? Here are some of the logistical considerations.

NPR.

https://www.npr.org/2023/03/31/1167447880/trump-

indictment-next-steps

Made in the USA
Coppell, TX
13 June 2023

18038777R00031